ŠTĚPÁNKA SEKANINOVÁ – AUTHOR

Why a book about poop? Because I've never met a kid who didn't start snickering when they heard the word *poop*. Basically, poop is just really funny. And when someone accidentally – if you'll pardon my French – farts, it usually makes those around them laugh rather than get offended. After all, professional flatulists (farters) of the past entertained the most noble of audiences ... and that's going back a long way. So I figured why not? Why not write a book about poops and farts and toilets and all that stuff? A book that is by its very nature lighthearted and yet, also by its very nature, surprisingly serious. In any case, I laughed myself silly when I was writing it. But I also learned a lot. So now, for example, I can tell for sure if I'm getting enough exercise or if I should be pushing myself a teensy bit more. And how do I know this? From my poop, of course ...

GROUNDED PIGEONS: MIROSLAVA GOMOLČÁKOVÁ & DANIEL HANDÁK – ILLUSTRATORS

We both studied graphic design, where we got to know each other and learned that we work really well together, and that's how our collaboration began. We'd both been drawing since we were little. Mirka was inspired by loads of great movies, while Daniel was mainly into computer games as a kid. The fact that we could also make a career in these two areas only occurred to us a bit later on in adulthood. So far we've mainly worked on films, TV series, and video games, and illustrating books is actually a bit of a new departure for us. Unlike animation and games, illustration is static, but we still try to get movement and various micro-stories in there.

The great thing about working as a duo is that you've got someone there to share all the funny sketches and situations that crop up when you're drawing (especially when you manage to draw something so bad it's brilliant) and also that you can always ask the other person for advice – for example, if you get stuck. You always get feedback. But the downside is that you always get feedback ... which sometimes can be really hard to accept :D

We'd advise budding illustrators to not be afraid of making mistakes, to try new things, and to give it your all, even if what you're drawing might at first look like ... well, a big old pile of poo.

POOPS AND FARTS
THE BOTTOM LINE

Written by Štěpánka Sekaninová
Illustrated by Miroslava Gomolčáková & Daniel Handák

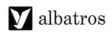

TABLE OF CONTENTS

BEFORE IT DROPS OUT OF US

There's quite a long process leading up to the moment when our poop drops out of us. It begins with hunger and some bites of food. The food we take in makes its way down to the stomach, where a chemical called hydrochloric acid swoops in and digests it. The digested food then journeys on down to the duodenum – the first part of the small intestine. There it's broken down further by pancreatic enzymes and bile produced by the liver, after which it can fully enter the small intestine. There proteins, carbohydrates, fats, and other substances are absorbed into the bloodstream. The ones that haven't been absorbed travel into the large intestine. And that's where they're turned into stool, which heads into the rectum and from there SPLAT ... PLOP ...

... into the toilet!

DID YOU KNOW ... ? THE UNDIGESTED REMAINS OF FOOD REPRESENT ONLY 50–80% OF POO. THE REST IS MADE UP OF GUT BACTERIA, WATER, AND BITS OF OUR OWN BODY TISSUE.

HOW MUCH DOES IT WEIGH?

On average we poo out a quarter of a pound to nearly half a pound of stool every day.

5

WHAT SHOULD IT LOOK LIKE?

Like a sausage about 4–5 inches long. But don't be alarmed if it's longer. That shows you have a healthy, balanced diet!

WHAT COLOR IS IT?

BROWN

Ideally a dark chocolate shade. This color is caused by dead red blood cells and bile.

BLACK

You've probably been feasting on blueberries, spinach, or other leafy vegetables. But sometimes black can be a sign of bleeding in the digestive tract, so if you see this color, tell an adult.

YELLOWY ORANGE

Uh-oh, your body seems to be having a hard time absorbing and processing fats.

ORANGE

For this shade of poo, you probably have carrots and apricots to thank – foods rich in an orange pigment called beta-carotene. Or it could be that most of your diet is dairy products.

GREEN

A green color is produced by leafy vegetables. It can also happen when food rushes through your digestive tract and into the large intestine too quickly. In other words, when you have diarrhea ...

GRAY

Points to a lack of bile pigments or what's called celiac disease.

RED

Yeah, well, what would you expect after eating beets, tomatoes, or watermelon?

WHEN YOU CAN'T GO ...

We should poop every day. But sometimes we don't need to and we can go for days before we get the urge. When the muscles in the large intestine contract too slowly, the stool moves more slowly and absorbs more water, making it harder and more difficult to push out.

... AND WHEN YOU CAN'T STOP GOING!

HEEEEEY! WHY DO YOU THINK I'M FREAKING OUT LIKE THIS WHEN THERE ISN'T EVEN A BAND PLAYING?!!!

The opposite of constipation is diarrhea – when we can't get off the toilet for even a minute. It's an intestinal disorder that involves excessive defecating. The poop is loose and frequent ... and there's too much of it!

9

WHAT HELPS WITH CONSTIPATION

YOGA

FIBER

EXERCISE

CASTOR OIL

OLIVE OIL

REGULAR FLUIDS

PRUNES OR PLUM COMPOTE

WHAT HELPS WITH DIARRHEA

PLAIN RICE
WITH CARROTS

AVOIDING
SWEETS

TURKEY – STEAMED
OR BOILED

POTATOES

BANANAS

CHAMOMILE OR
BLACK TEA

BLUEBERRIES AND
BLACKCURRANTS

11

TYPES OF POO

The shape of our poo says a lot about us. So much so that a team of gastroenterologists (gut health experts) from Bristol University in the United Kingdom created the BRISTOL STOOL SCALE, which describes the seven basic types of poo and explains the health reasons for their shape. Experts are able to tell from a person's poo how their digestive and excretory system is working. They can even use stools to work out whether or not food supplements and medicines agree with the human body and how it copes with a lack of movement or, on the contrary, responds to exercise. And to think – we turn our noses up at poo!

1 HARD LUMPS
Typical constipation

 4 SMOOTH, SOFT SAUSAGE
Bravo! Couldn't be better!

 5 SOFT PIECES
Uh-oh, mild diarrhea

BRISTOL STOOL SCALE

  LUMPY SAUSAGE
Time to clean those bowels out!

  SAUSAGE WITH CRACKS
Ideal state

  MUSHY PIECES
Full-blown diarrhea!

  LIQUID
Really bad diarrhea!

13

WHAT A GREAT COFFEE!

One of the best coffees is made from the droppings of civets – cat-like creatures that feast on coffee cherries. The beans are then fermented in their stomachs, and when the time comes the civets poop them out. And that's the moment all those gourmets are waiting for, because the fermented beans give the drink a delectable flavour. Another delicacy is coffee made from beans that have passed through the digestive tract of an elephant. It's less bitter and tastes like chocolate and cherries.

PANDAS POOPING

Pandas spend their whole lives eating, pooping, and sleeping – and not much else! This is reflected in how often they have bowel movements. They go for a number two as many as 40 times a day.

I'M HUNGRY!

It's normal for baby rabbits to feast on their mother's poo. They get important gut bacteria from it that help them to create their own gut microbiome.

EXPLOSIVE DROPPINGS

Bat droppings contain potassium nitrate, which is explosive. That's why bat droppings were used to make explosives and gunpowder during the First World War.

AS FAR AS YOU CAN

Hippos are real hotshots compared to penguins. They're in a different league and can happily fire their droppings like a canon – up to a distance of 30 feet!

CHECK IT OUT: CUBES!

Australian marsupials called wombats like to stand out from the crowd – by pooping in the shape of small cubes! They can easily produce a hundred of them in a single night. They then collect them and place them around their territory as a warning to unwelcome visitors but also a way to attract a potential mate. The advantage of the cube is obvious – it simply can't roll away.

FIRE IN THE HOLE!

The pressure from a little penguin's bottom is so powerful it can launch its poop up to 4 feet away.

GOLD FEVER

Believe it or not, human feces also contain tiny traces of precious metals – gold, silver, and palladium. Now we just need to figure out how to extract them from our poos and we can all be rich!

THE GREATEST TREASURE

For archeologists, coming across our ancestors' excrement on a dig is a major event. By analyzing it, they can tell what people ate back in ancient times and how healthy their diet was.

BIO-PROPULSION

In 2015, the very first bio-bus went into operation in Britain. The vehicle was powered by biomethane, a gas produced during the treatment of sewage and food waste. This kind of bus doesn't pollute the air – it's totally clean. Pretty ironic since it runs on poop, eh?

POOP ON A PLATE

In China, toilets have proved so inspiring that a special themed restaurant opened in the capital city where you eat your lunch or dinner sitting on a toilet bowl. The dish you're served will look like a big helping of you-know-what ... but you can chow down with a clear conscience – it only looks like something filthy.

A HISTORY OF THE TOILET

Where did our ancient ancestors go to the bathroom? Probably in the bushes or behind a tree. Job done. But that all changed when people started moving from the countryside into towns. They couldn't just poop all over the pavement. That's when the first toilets became necessary.

MESOPOTAMIA

The ancient Sumerians pooped in a civilized manner. Their toilets looked like brick chairs covered with water-repellent cloth and located over a cesspit. When Mesopotamians relieved themselves, their number twos would drop through a gap into clay pipes and then be whooshed away into a cesspit.

ANCIENT EGYPT

Rich Egyptians' toilets were made of limestone, while the poor had to make do with a wooden stool with a hole cut out of it. Back then, they could only dream of running water, so they flushed away their excrement with buckets of water. And where did it all end up? Either in the street or in the Nile River.

MINOAN CULTURE

The Minoan palaces on the island of Crete were all decked out with advanced flushing toilets. Since we're talking about a civilization that existed 4,000 years ago, we have to salute its engineers. The Minoan toilet was actually a wooden seat located above a pipe. Water flowed through this pipe from a tank on the roof into an underground sewer.

ROME

The Ancient Romans enjoyed comfortable latrines where they could answer the call of nature while holding serious discussions or making important deals. (Talk about mixing business with pleasure!) The products of their digestion dropped into channels with continuous streams of running water, which also flowed through a gutter beside the toilet bench.

THE MIDDLE AGES

Forget sewage systems and state-of-the-art hygiene. The contents of medieval chamber pots were simply dumped in the street. If there was no chamber pot around, people would relieve themselves wherever they were – even in the corner of a room. Basically, our medieval ancestors didn't care, so long as their stomach stopped hurting.

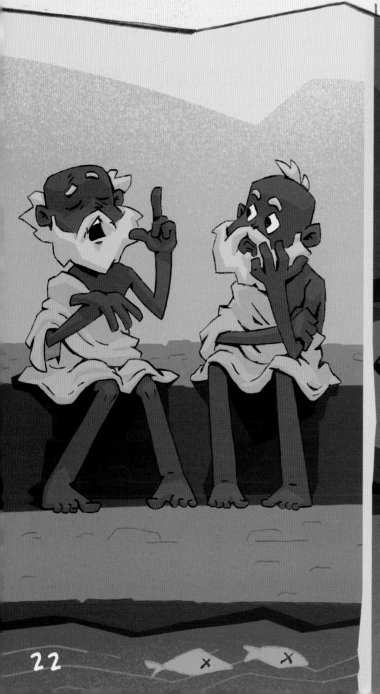

THE PRIVY

The owners of castles enjoyed the luxury of a castle toilet, known as a privy or garderobe. In reality, this was just a small, uncomfortable seat with a hole in it straight above the castle's moat. To cover up the squishy sounds of defecating from the privy alcove – and God forbid someone should fart – there was often live music to accompany the lord as he pooped.

FROM A CHAIR TO A FLUSH TOILET

The Renaissance brought a bit of comfort to bowel movements. People would poop sitting in a chair with a built-in chamber pot. The first flush toilet saw the light of day at the end of the 18th century. At first, this innovation was only for the rich. Ordinary people still had to make do – and make *doo* – with a chamber pot.

23

WHAT ELSE DO PEOPLE DO WHILE SITTING ON THE TOILET?

MEDITATE

READ

LISTEN TO MUSIC

SCROLL THROUGH SOCIAL MEDIA

STARE INTO SPACE

THE BASIC TYPES OF TOILETS:

A FLUSH TOILET
A toilet bowl with a flush – very common in Europe and North America.

A SQUAT TOILET
Either an ordinary hole in the ground or a flushing device that looks like a container sunk into the ground. Particularly popular in Asia.

A DRY TOILET
Just an ordinary hole in the ground.

A CHILD'S POTTY.

WHAT DID OUR ANCESTORS WIPE THEIR BOTTOMS WITH?

Leaves

Whatever they had on hand. And the results were mixed. Imagine the scene. No matter how hard you search, the only thing within reach is a stone. Well, if there's nothing else for it ... In short, there were all kinds of substitutes for toilet paper. Some were soft and gentle, others sharp, and the worst ones unspeakable. What would all those who had to wipe their backside with ceramic shards have given for a piece of toilet paper?!

Moss

Snow

Ceramic shards

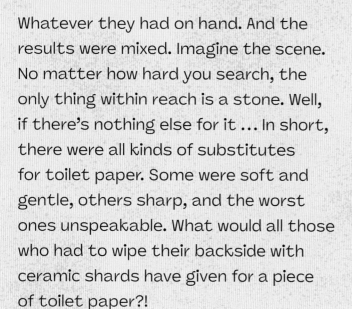

Sheep's wool

Cloth wrapped around bamboo

Sand

Grass

Stones

Wooden stick

Dirt

Printed paper

Rounded terracotta fragments (*pessoi*)

Corn cobs

A sea sponge on a stick

27

A HISTORY OF TOILET PAPER

1. Toilet paper first began to be used in China around the year 589 AD.

2. This innovation was slow to catch on in the rest of the world, but by the 16th century even Europeans were getting used to wiping their backsides with paper. The printing press was to thank for this – what else could you do with unusable printed sheets?

3. From the 17th century onward, people made use of old newspapers.

4. In 1857 an American named Joseph C. Gayetty came up with the first industrially produced toilet paper, made from Manila hemp infused with aloe vera extract. And to make sure the spiritual father of this amazing toilet paper wouldn't be forgotten, each sheet of paper had his name on it.

5. Shortly after this, America came up with another innovation: toilet paper on a roll!

6. The first European toilet-paper factory opened in Germany in 1928 and its owner's name was Hans Klenk. At first his toilet paper was said to feel terrible, like sandpaper. Fortunately, Hans Klenk later came up with a fancy new toilet paper – a type that didn't scratch but was velvety soft.

7. The year 1942 saw the launch of the first two-ply toilet paper.

8. This was followed by colored toilet paper in 1957 and moist toilet paper or wet wipes in the 1990s – when life became beautiful!

POOPING OUTDOORS

Pooing in the great outdoors? Glorious! Relieving yourself in the pine-scented shade of the forest is heavenly. But if loads of people go traipsing around the countryside and every other nature lover leaves behind their half pound of poop, it becomes a serious problem! Human poop takes a whole year to decompose!

That's why popular national parks give visitors special poo bags containing a substance that transforms excrement into a chemically inactive gel that doesn't smell.

OK, BUT IF YOU'VE REALLY GOT TO GO, WHAT CAN YOU DO TO AVOID CONTAMINATING THE LANDSCAPE?

70 STEPS

1

Walk at least 70 steps away from any path or water source.

2

Find a spot near some thick undergrowth or on a slope.

6–8 INCHES

4–6 INCHES

3

Pick an elevated area that gets sunlight for faster decomposition.

4

Dig a hole about 6–8 inches deep and 4–6 inches wide. Do your business in it and then fill it in.

5

If you are near a river canyon, a mountain, or a beach, it's best to take your poop away with you.

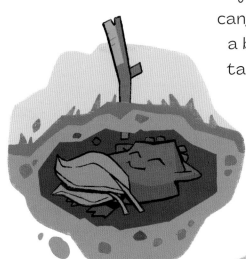

CHOOSE WHITE, UNPERFUMED, BIO-DEGRADABLE TOILET PAPER. THEN YOU CAN BURY IT – OR, EVEN BETTER, TAKE IT AWAY FROM THE FOREST WITH YOU!

POOPING IN ANTARCTICA

Even in the freezing Antarctic weather, we still have to answer the call of nature. When you've gotta go, you've gotta go, even if it means having to struggle out of several layers of trousers and puffer jackets before sitting down on a bucket designed for pooping in.

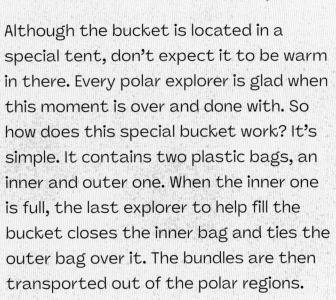

Although the bucket is located in a special tent, don't expect it to be warm in there. Every polar explorer is glad when this moment is over and done with. So how does this special bucket work? It's simple. It contains two plastic bags, an inner and outer one. When the inner one is full, the last explorer to help fill the bucket closes the inner bag and ties the outer bag over it. The bundles are then transported out of the polar regions.

YIKES, A STORM!

The special toilet tents for number ones and twos can even stand up to harsh polar storms. That's because they're secured to the ice by sturdy pegs. Nothing beats a bit of privacy.

HEEELP!

But what if a polar explorer needs to go when they're far away from the tent? Then they have to find a sheltered spot to go in or dig a hole in the snow. It's no picnic. Just you try it in the freezing cold!

33

POOPING IN SPACE

HOUSTON, WE HAVE A PROBLEM.

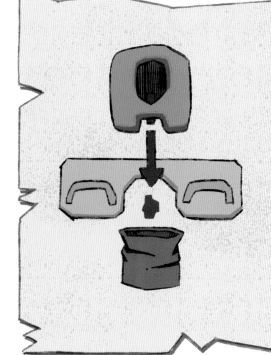

There are even toilets in space. At first sight they look like the ones here on Earth, but they're decked out with foot restraints and a seat that snugly fits against the astronaut's bottom. But before they get down to business, the astronaut has to fit a special bag into the toilet to catch everything. When it's all over, the bag with its "treasure" is sealed and stored in a container. After a few days, the contents of the container are emptied out. So we might think we're seeing a shooting star when it's actually a big ole bag of frozen feces.

It took engineers a long time to design such a perfect, functional toilet for astronauts. Before they did, those space-farers had no choice but to poop into diapers, plastic bags – whatever worked.

CURED BY POOP

People suffering from some diseases have feces from healthy people transplanted into their intestines. That's because they're packed with useful bacteria. And, lo and behold, almost 98% of the sick are cured. Then they can go about their business with new, high-quality gut flora.

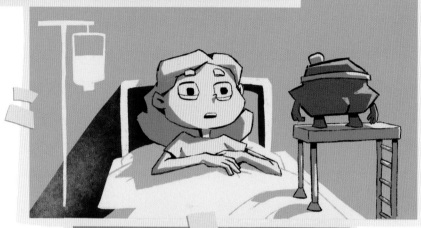

WHY DOES HUMAN POOP STINK?

Evolution arranged it that way to keep us from eating feces full of bacteria and microorganisms that are harmful to our health. Clever, eh?

A GOOD SNIFF SHOULD DO THE TRICK!

Struggling to drop a biggie? Sniff a new book and it'll be smooth sailing! Seriously – this is called the Mariko Aoki phenomenon and it's named after a Japanese woman who described it in the 1990s.

But be careful, though – it might just be a myth. No scientist has yet succeeded in proving a connection between the smell of books and the urge to go number two.

DID YOU KNOW THAT A PERSON PRODUCES TWICE AS MUCH STOOL IN A YEAR AS THEY THEMSELVES WEIGH?

FARTS

A fart – aka flatuence – is a mixture of gases produced in our digestive tract when food breaks down, combined with air we have swallowed. When you throw gut bacteria and chemical reactions from gastric juices into the mix, it all adds up to a great big classic fart! And thank goodness it does. Farting is proof that everything is working properly. On average, a healthy person releases their intestinal gases into the world up to 14 times a day!

TRAPPED WIND

Sometimes a fart just won't come out. Basically, the way out of the digestive tract has been blocked. Gradually, more and more farts come along, and before long the poor person's belly is swollen like a balloon and ever so painful!

THE BEST THING FOR TRAPPED GAS: A STOMACH MASSAGE!

OR YOU CAN TRY:

HERBAL TEA

YOGA

WALKING

A RICH FLATULIST

A flatulist is a person who has such control over their bowels that they can fart on demand. Flatulists used to perform at royal courts, merrily farting in front of the king and his retinue. One such flatulist was Roland the Farter, who lived in England in the 12th century and was one of the favorites of King Henry II. The highlight of his act, which was a hit at Christmas parties, consisted of one jump, a whistle, and a final fart. All of this earned Roland a manor in Suffolk with 30 acres of land.

IRELAND

Staying in the 12th century but moving a little further west, in Ireland there were professional farters known as *braigetóirs*. They toured the courts of the aristocracy, entertaining those present with their barking bottoms.

JAPAN

Even Japan had its professional farters, known as *heppiri otoko*, who took part in farting contests, as is recorded in scrolls by an artist from the Edo period (1603–1867).

FRANCE

Le Pétomane, whose real name was Joseph Pujol (1857–1945), was another famous and successful artist who entertained the public by ripping farts.

43

DO ANIMALS FART TOO?

We have no reason to be ashamed of ourselves! We're not the only ones on planet Earth who relieve themselves by farting, breaking wind, and letting one rip. Rest assured, animals fart too.

AND THE WINNER OF THE FARTIEST BEAST IN THE WORLD COMPETITION IS: THE TERMITE! IN SECOND PLACE THE CAMEL, AND IN THIRD PLACE IS THE ZEBRA. IN THE LEAGUE TABLE OF THE BIGGEST FARTERS, WE HUMANS ONLY COME IN EIGHTH – AFTER DOGS!

Sloths go about it in a different way. Although gases are produced in their intestines, instead of thundering out of their anus they are absorbed into their bloodstream and then breathed out.

As for birds, they don't fart at all. They digest their food very quickly and so their intestines don't contain the bacteria responsible for the production of gases.

WATCH OUT, HERE COMES A CHEETAH! YOU'D BETTER HOPE IT DOESN'T FART, CAUSE A CHEETAH'S TOOTS ARE EXCEPTIONALLY STINKY.

JURASSIC FART

CAUSE OF CLIMATE CHANGE REVEALED?

Gigantic dinosaurs farted so much that they were capable of releasing as much as 520 million tons of methane into the atmosphere each year. Methane is a gas which is notorious for contributing to global warning. Experts have thought about this and come to the conclusion that the farty species of giant reptile may have been responsible for global climate change in the Mesozoic era.

Just imagine those huge dinosaur monsters and their guts. What must it have been like when one of those enormous creatures relieved its bloated belly – let alone when many farts came from a whole herd of Tyrannosaurs, Brachiosaurs, Stegosaurs, and other "sauruses"? Global catastrophe was imminent!

46

CAN FARTS BURN? OF COURSE THEY CAN! AFTER ALL, THEY'RE FORMED OF MANY FLAMMABLE GASES.

Herrings use farting as a way of communicating with each other. They can modify the sound of their bowels across a range of up to three octaves, depending on what they want to say.

I'M FARTING I LOVE YOU!

POOPS AND FARTS
THE BOTTOM LINE

© B4U Publishing for Albatros,
an imprint of Albatros Media Group, 2025
5. května 1746/22, Prague 4,
Czech Republic.

Author: Štěpánka Sekaninová
Illustrations: © Miroslava
Gomolčáková & Daniel Handák
(Grounded Pigeons) 2024

ŠTĚPÁNKA

DAN & MIRKA

Editors: Tom Velčovský,
Štěpánka Sekaninová
Translators: Graeme and
Suzanne Dibble
Proofreader: Scott Alexander Jones
Graphics and typesetting:
Martin Urbánek

Printed in
China by Leo Paper Group Ltd.
www.albatrosbooks.com

TOM

MARTIN

albatros

WOULD YOU LIKE TO LEARN MORE?

Everyone Poops by Taro Gomi; Kane Miller, 1993.

A Bathroom Book for People Not Pooping or Peeing but Using the Bathroom as an Escape by Joe Pera; Forge Books, 2021.

It Takes Guts: How Your Body Turns Food Into Fuel (and Poop) by Dr. Jennifer Gardy; Greystone Kids, 2021.

THE WORD POOP IN ANOTHER TEN LANGUAGES

"THE MORE LANGUAGES YOU KNOW, THE MORE YOU ARE HUMAN."